The Essential Author Log

Alexis Donkin

DEDICATION

For all aspiring authors everywhere, because I know how it is.

CONTENTS

ACKNOWLEDGMENTS

Thank you to my family and tireless supporters, without whom, I would never have the strength to press onward. I am also grateful for my doubts and fears, without which I would never have gained the strength to continue this pursuit.

INTRODUCTION

Congratulations! You're on your way to realizing your writing and publishing dreams! How do I know? Because you took the first step and purchased this log. You understand something fundamental: the unique power of using a pen to write goals.

The pen uses something that clicking keys does not – muscle memory. By writing your goals and the steps to achieve them, you write them into your brain. That tactile action inscribes not only in ink on paper, but in the mind and heart. This is the power of the pen. This is why, ultimately, you are more likely to complete the tasks set before you – because they are *on your mind*.

It took me a long time to start writing. I was convinced writers could never be successful, and more than that, I believed it was impossible for me to finish a book. I thought I didn't have the patience, discipline, or skill. I thought I was doomed to failure, but I decided to give it a try because I was unemployed and had nothing to lose.

Then something remarkable happened – I finished a book. Not only did I finish, but I finished writing the first draft in a week. That's all it took. A week.

The problem was that kind of work schedule was unsustainable. I spent 15 hours straight writing. I woke in the middle of the night to do research. I had to remind myself to take breaks to eat, pee, or sleep. It was insane. I would finish writing only to enter reality in a disassociated state. I couldn't be sure what was real – the world of my book, or the world around me. I couldn't do that all the time because it was extremely unhealthy. Besides, writing is only a small portion of what is necessary to succeed as any kind of author,, but especially independent authors.

I needed balance – within my work and my life. I needed to institute boundaries and variety. Through studying business professionals, success coaches, and successful writers, I cobbled together systems and exercises to establish a healthy level of balance that would allow me to reach my goals. I discovered that if I spent a little bit of time every day on my goals, I was more likely to complete them.

If I came up with annual goals, monthly goals, and then divided them into bite-sized chunks, they were very manageable. In fact, they were easy. *Anyone could do this!*

Unfortunately, few people realize how easy this is to do. Thus in an effort to help others realize their writing and publishing dreams, I decided to share these systems in an easy step-by-step log. That's right. You just follow the steps outlined in this log and track your goals. By doing that, *you will see results.*

Keep in mind – your goal needs to be achievable. If you've never written an essay then you *probably* won't be writing the next international best-seller, *but* you *can* write a novel. If you've never written a screenplay, you *probably* aren't going to get Steven Spielberg to produce your movie (at least not right away!). It needs to be a realistic goal – something that is a little bit of a reach, but is still doable. This could be to get published in a literary magazine, to apply to a grant, finish a manuscript, or start and maintain a blog. If you want to finish a novel or that memoir you always wanted to write, this log will help you.

Keep in mind, writing is a skill, *not* a talent. This means anyone can learn to write well with committed practice. In his book, *Outliers,* Malcolm Gladwell wrote that it takes 10,000 hours to master something. Likewise, it's been said that to become an international expert in something,, you should read for 2,555 hours (about 1 hour daily for 7 years).

On August 30, 2010 I decided I wanted to be a writer. I know this because I started a blog called "A Musing Alexis" that day and declared my intention. Guess what? In five years I've done more than 10,000 hours writing and more than 2,555 hours reading about my craft - all thanks to the systems in this log!

Now you're wondering, if all this is so easy, how come everyone doesn't do it? It's simple. There is an X factor – persistence. Disciplined persistence is key to achieving writing goals. This log makes it easier to stay disciplined because it has everything in one place and gives you easy to follow steps *however,* having this log does *not* guarantee success. **You are responsible for achieving your goals**. You control how much you are willing and able to do.

Through this log, I will walk you through determining the next six months of your efforts (it sounds scary now – but trust me, you can do this!). You will brainstorm where you want to be at the end of that time and then break down your efforts into monthly goals. You'll convert each monthly goal into 4 weekly goals and then daily tasks. At the end of the six months, you'll have 2 weeks of respite where you will have an opportunity to revisit your longterm vision and plan your next series of goals.

I know that sounds intimidating, but stay with me on this.

If you really want to write, you need to commit or get real with yourself. Is this a hobby? That's fine. You still want to figure out how to maintain a blog and this log will help you. Is writing an undying passion you *need* to turn it into a career? Then you definitely want to use the systems in this book. Either way, if you follow all the guidelines I've provided, your writing craft will be transformed.

I know this because I did it and I believe you can too.

GOAL SETTING

Before you start transforming your writing, it is important to decide what you want your writing to look like. Sometimes this can involve a long term plan, or it can be much shorter.

For some, especially aspiring professionals, it may be easier to start with five years. For others, like the hobbyist, you have a clear path for the next six months. If you're already set with your six month goal, then skip ahead to "The Six Month Goal" exercise. If not, then work through the "5 Year Plan" below.

The 5 Year Plan

1. **Where do you want to be in five years with your writing?** Get very specific about what this involves (i.e. book signings, appearances, sales, etc). Think about promotion, publication, social media, sales etc. Let's take an example of someone who wants to join a writer's association. They would have to fulfill all the requirements for membership (royalties, certain number of publications etc) which would likely include other kinds of things, such as regular book tours or conference panels.

_____

_____

_____

_____

_____

2. **What steps will you take to get there?** What will need to be in place? Get specific. For example, if you want to be a member of the Science-fiction and Fantasy Writers Association, you need to have published X stories in paying markets or have a self-published title that has earned over $X in royalties. To achieve this you need to have a certain number of polished stories and then pitch them to different magazines and or have a completed and published title that has sold so many copies.

_____

_____

_____

_____

_____

_____

_____

_____

_____

3. **Divide these into 5 yearly goals**. In the above example, perhaps this year should be focused on writing short stories and or finishing your novel. Another goal might be to find a successful author to mentor you, or join a writer's group to hone your craft. Don't worry about getting too in depth. We'll do that in just a moment!

1. _____

   _____

2. _____

   _____

3. _____

   _____

4. _____

   _____

5. _____

   _____

4. Now that you have your big plan developed, unpack your goal for this year. **Divide this into two parts – one for the first six months and one for the second.**

    1. _____

       _____

    2. _____

       _____

The Six Month Goal

Take your six month goal and **write it here as though it has already happened:**

_____

_____

_____

_____

_____

Now that you have your six month goal, you can divide it into smaller monthly chunks. When you see your goals divided this way, it becomes a lot easier to see how bigger goals can be achieved.

Keep in mind, this log includes touching five different aspects of writing daily, so you may want to address multiple aspects in your monthly goals. Be sure your goals are reasonable given time constraints and your work style.

Some people may struggle to complete 500 words daily with a full 8 hours devoted to writing, while others can pump out 10,000 in the same amount of time. Start out small and adjust as you go. While you have written your goal down, do not feel tied to it. It is okay to adjust and tweak as needed. Ultimately you want to be successful and feel as though you have accomplished something. This process should never be a punishment or an exercise in self-denigration.

For example, at one point I had a daily word count goal of 4000 words. Simultaneously I was caring for a baby which meant nursing, changing diapers, and rescuing him from himself. This goal of 4000 words may have been very achievable when I didn't have an infant, but with one, it was impossible. I dropped my goal to 2000. That was touch and go. I dropped it again to 1000 words. Some days I *just* scrounged that number, while others, I was able to get 2500 to 4000 words in a burst of inspiration (or babysitting!). I went from feeling like a failure to feeling like I could successfully publish. It made a huge difference in my productivity and overall perspective.

Recognizing this, be gentle and realistic with yourself when making your monthly goals. I left space for specific goals (and daily tasks) in the following areas:

- Writing – includes blogging, guest posting, word counts, rewriting, and editing.
- Social media – means posting, commenting, sharing in your selected networks.
- Promotion – could be blog tours, advertising, contests, quizzes, giveaways, graphics etc.
- Publishing – includes formatting, cover art, categorization, distribution, etc.
- Other – I include reading and continuing education here, but there may be other possibilities you want to include (conferences, networking, mastermind groups, self-work etc).

Now write your six *general* monthly goals here and when you get to that month in the log, you can get more specific (and write your "goal reality statement").

Month 1 Goal:

_____

_____

_____

Month 2 Goal:

_____

_____

_____

Month 3 Goal:

_____

_____

_____

Month 4 Goal:

_____

_____

_____

Month 5 Goal:

_____

_____

_____

Month 6 Goal:

_____

_____

_____

MONTH 1

Below write down your month 1 goals in the following areas as needed.

Writing:

_____

_____

Social media:

_____

_____

Promotion:

_____

_____

Publishing:

_____

_____

Other:

_____

_____

Monthly goal statement (written as though it is reality):

_____

_____

_____

_____

_____

_____

Week 1

Take a few minutes now to portion out your monthly goal into weekly goals. If you intend to write a short story this month, perhaps this week is spent writing, where next week will involve editing.

In the example of this particular writing goal, you would decide how many words you intend to complete daily – say a minimum of 500 words until story completion. This would give you 3500 words at the end of the week if you followed this amount every day. That number is higher than most magazines accept, but it gives you a good amount of wiggle room for editing in week 2.

Week 1 Goal:

_____

_____

_____

Weekly thought:

The first step is often the hardest. Already you've clarified your goals for the next few months which is more than most people ever do! Congratulations! You're already better prepared and disciplined than most!

Monday Checklist:

☐Writing_____
_____

☐ Social media (15 min per 2-3 of following: Twit FB G+ LI Pin
_____

☐ Promotion strategies/tactics
_____

☐ Publishing progress post/article/book
_____

☐ Other (in exchange for one of the above)
_____

Notes:_____
_____
_____
_____
_____

Tuesday Checklist:

☐Writing_____
_____

☐ Social media (15 min per 2-3 of following: Twit FB G+ LI Pin
_____

☐ Promotion strategies/tactics
_____

☐ Publishing progress post/article/book
_____

☐ Other (in exchange for one of the above)
_____

Notes:_____
_____
_____
_____

Wednesday Checklist:

☐Writing_____

☐ Social media (15 min per 2-3 of following: Twit FB G+ LI Pin

☐ Promotion strategies/tactics

☐ Publishing progress post/article/book

☐ Other (in exchange for one of the above)

Notes:_____
_____
_____
_____

Thursday Checklist:

☐Writing_____

☐ Social media (15 min per 2-3 of following: Twit FB G+ LI Pin

☐ Promotion strategies/tactics

☐ Publishing progress post/article/book

☐ Other (in exchange for one of the above)

Notes:_____
_____
_____
_____

Friday Checklist:

☐ Writing _____

_____

☐ Social media (15 min per 2-3 of following: Twit FB G+ LI Pin

_____

☐ Promotion strategies/tactics

_____

☐ Publishing progress post/article/book

_____

☐ Other (in exchange for one of the above)

_____

Notes:_____

_____

_____

_____

Saturday Checklist:

☐ Writing _____

_____

☐ Social media (15 min per 2-3 of following: Twit FB G+ LI Pin

_____

☐ Promotion strategies/tactics

_____

☐ Publishing progress post/article/book

_____

☐ Other (in exchange for one of the above)

_____

Notes:

_____

_____

_____

_____

Sunday-Funday!

Everyone needs a scheduled break. While this log includes six working days, everyone's work life is different. Some may need to have two "fundays" and that would be perfectly fine. Make a real effort to *not* write today. The only thing you *might* do today is the below weekly assessment. You worked hard all week. You deserve a little fun!

Week 1 Goal Assessment:

☐ achieved
☐ partially achieved

If not completed, why?

_____

What can you change next week to achieve your goal? Or alternatively, if you achieved your goal, do you need to make any adjustments? If so, what?

_____

_____

_____

Week 2

This week's goal may need to be adjusted considering what you completed last week. You may have discovered you are an overachiever – or maybe you had a really difficult week because of things outside your control. Whatever the case, choose your goal accordingly. Always be gentle and realistic!

Week 2 Goal:

_____
_____
_____

Weekly thought:

You're starting to get a routine. Your excitement about using your log is still high even though you have just begun to see some results. Keep working at it! You'll be amazed at what you can accomplish!

Monday Checklist:

☐ Writing_____

☐ Social media (15 min per 2-3 of following: Twit FB G+ LI Pin

☐ Promotion strategies/tactics

☐ Publishing progress post/article/book

☐ Other (in exchange for one of the above)

Notes:_____
_____
_____
_____
_____

Tuesday Checklist:

☐ Writing_____

☐ Social media (15 min per 2-3 of following: Twit FB G+ LI Pin

☐ Promotion strategies/tactics

☐ Publishing progress post/article/book

☐ Other (in exchange for one of the above)

Notes:_____
_____
_____
_____

Wednesday Checklist:

☐ Writing_____

☐ Social media (15 min per 2-3 of following: Twit FB G+ LI Pin

☐ Promotion strategies/tactics

☐ Publishing progress post/article/book

☐ Other (in exchange for one of the above)

Notes:_____
_____
_____
_____

Thursday Checklist:

☐ Writing_____

☐ Social media (15 min per 2-3 of following: Twit FB G+ LI Pin

☐ Promotion strategies/tactics

☐ Publishing progress post/article/book

☐ Other (in exchange for one of the above)

Notes:_____
_____
_____
_____

Friday Checklist:

☐ Writing_____

_____

☐ Social media (15 min per 2-3 of following: Twit FB G+ LI Pin

_____

☐ Promotion strategies/tactics

_____

☐ Publishing progress post/article/book

_____

☐ Other (in exchange for one of the above)

_____

Notes:_____

_____

_____

_____

Saturday Checklist:

☐ Writing_____

_____

☐ Social media (15 min per 2-3 of following: Twit FB G+ LI Pin

_____

☐ Promotion strategies/tactics

_____

☐ Publishing progress post/article/book

_____

☐ Other (in exchange for one of the above)

_____

Notes:

_____

_____

_____

_____

Sunday-Funday!

Have you come up for air? Make a real effort to *not* write today. The only thing you *might* do today is the below weekly assessment. You worked hard all week. You deserve a little fun!

Week 2 Goal Assessment:

☐ achieved
☐ partially achieved

If not completed, why?

_____

What can you change next week to achieve your goal? Or alternatively, if you achieved your goal, do you need to make any adjustments? If so, what?

_____

_____

_____

Week 3

You should start to see some real results even though you're only in week 3. By now, you may have some work completed, and possibly you've made some connections. This week may be the first time you're really confronted by difficult tasks, such as researching literary magazines for submissions or creating spreadsheets to track your submissions. While these aren't the fun parts of writing, they are necessary to help you achieve your goals.

Week 3 Goal:

_____

_____

_____

Weekly thought:

With all the results you're seeing, you may be tempted to push yourself too hard. DON'T! It is better to pace yourself. This is a marathon – not a sprint. Plan accordingly!

Monday Checklist:

☐ Writing _____

_____

☐ Social media (15 min per 2-3 of following: Twit FB G+ LI Pin

_____

☐ Promotion strategies/tactics

_____

☐ Publishing progress post/article/book

_____

☐ Other (in exchange for one of the above)

_____

Notes: _____

_____

_____

_____

_____

Tuesday Checklist:

☐ Writing _____

_____

☐ Social media (15 min per 2-3 of following: Twit FB G+ LI Pin

_____

☐ Promotion strategies/tactics

_____

☐ Publishing progress post/article/book

_____

☐ Other (in exchange for one of the above)

_____

Notes: _____

_____

_____

_____

_____

Wednesday Checklist:

☐ Writing_____

☐ Social media (15 min per 2-3 of following: Twit FB G+ LI Pin

☐ Promotion strategies/tactics

☐ Publishing progress post/article/book

☐ Other (in exchange for one of the above)

Notes:_____
_____
_____
_____

Thursday Checklist:

☐ Writing_____

☐ Social media (15 min per 2-3 of following: Twit FB G+ LI Pin

☐ Promotion strategies/tactics

☐ Publishing progress post/article/book

☐ Other (in exchange for one of the above)

Notes:_____
_____
_____
_____

Friday Checklist:

☐ Writing _____

☐ Social media (15 min per 2-3 of following: Twit FB G+ LI Pin
_____

☐ Promotion strategies/tactics
_____

☐ Publishing progress post/article/book
_____

☐ Other (in exchange for one of the above)
_____

Notes:_____
_____
_____
_____

Saturday Checklist:

☐ Writing _____

☐ Social media (15 min per 2-3 of following: Twit FB G+ LI Pin
_____

☐ Promotion strategies/tactics
_____

☐ Publishing progress post/article/book
_____

☐ Other (in exchange for one of the above)
_____

Notes:
_____
_____
_____
_____

Sunday-Funday!

Maybe you should curl up on the couch and binge watch your favorite television series. Whatever you do, make a real effort to *not* write today. The only thing you *might* do today is the below weekly assessment. You worked hard all week. You deserve a little fun!

Week 3 Goal Assessment:

☐ achieved
☐ partially achieved

If not completed, why?

_____

What can you change next week to achieve your goal? Or alternatively, if you achieved your goal, do you need to make any adjustments? If so, what?

_____

_____

_____

Week 4

You've already done so much. Take a moment to breathe and look at how far you've come in such a short time. What is left to do to accomplish your monthly goals? Be sure to push as you need in order to reach them. You want to feel successful, but be careful you don't fry your brain (or motivation!) in the process!

Week 4 Goal:

_____

_____

_____

Weekly thought:

This is the last week in your monthly goal! At the end of this week, you'll be approximately 16% finished with your 6 month goal. Isn't that wild? That might not seem like very much, but trust me – it is huge! Every day you're doing more, getting better, and growing closer to where you want to be! Keep working and you'll get there!

Monday Checklist:

☐ Writing_____

_____

☐ Social media (15 min per 2-3 of following: Twit FB G+ LI Pin

_____

☐ Promotion strategies/tactics

_____

☐ Publishing progress post/article/book

_____

☐ Other (in exchange for one of the above)

_____

Notes:_____

_____

_____

_____

_____

Tuesday Checklist:

☐ Writing_____

_____

☐ Social media (15 min per 2-3 of following: Twit FB G+ LI Pin

_____

☐ Promotion strategies/tactics

_____

☐ Publishing progress post/article/book

_____

☐ Other (in exchange for one of the above)

_____

Notes:_____

_____

_____

_____

Wednesday Checklist:

☐Writing_____

☐ Social media (15 min per 2-3 of following: Twit FB G+ LI Pin

☐ Promotion strategies/tactics

☐ Publishing progress post/article/book

☐ Other (in exchange for one of the above)

Notes:_____
_____
_____
_____

Thursday Checklist:

☐Writing_____

☐ Social media (15 min per 2-3 of following: Twit FB G+ LI Pin

☐ Promotion strategies/tactics

☐ Publishing progress post/article/book

☐ Other (in exchange for one of the above)

Notes:_____
_____
_____
_____

Friday Checklist:

☐ Writing_____

☐ Social media (15 min per 2-3 of following: Twit FB G+ LI Pin

☐ Promotion strategies/tactics

☐ Publishing progress post/article/book

☐ Other (in exchange for one of the above)

Notes:_____

_____

_____

Saturday Checklist:

☐ Writing_____

☐ Social media (15 min per 2-3 of following: Twit FB G+ LI Pin

☐ Promotion strategies/tactics

☐ Publishing progress post/article/book

☐ Other (in exchange for one of the above)

Notes:

_____

_____

_____

Sunday-Funday!

When was the last time you played billiards? Went boot-scootin'? Just don't write today. The only things you *might* do today are the weekly and monthly assessments. You worked hard all week. You deserve a little fun!

Week 4 Goal Assessment:

☐ achieved
☐ partially achieved

If not completed, why?

_____

What can you change next week to achieve your goal? Or alternatively, if you achieved your goal, do you need to make any adjustments? If so, what?

_____

_____

_____

Month 1 Goal Assessment:

☐ achieved
☐ partially achieved

If not completed, why?

_____

What can you change next week to achieve your goal? Or alternatively, if you achieved your goal, do you need to make any adjustments? If so, what?

_____

_____

_____

MONTH 2

Below write down your month 2 goals in the following areas as needed.

Writing:
_____
_____

Social media:
_____
_____

Promotion:
_____
_____

Publishing:
_____
_____

Other:
_____
_____

Monthly goal statement (written as though it is reality):
_____
_____
_____
_____
_____
_____
_____

Week 1

Take a few minutes now to portion out your monthly goal into weekly goals. If you intend to begin a blog this month, perhaps this week is spent designing the blog.

In the example of this particular goal, you might work on layout one day, graphics another, determine widgets or plug-ins another. Each day would bring you closer to completion of the blog until at the end of the week, your blog is ready for content! This way in week 2, you will be prepared to post interesting information and ideas for your readers.

Week 1 Goal:

_____

_____

_____

Weekly thought:

It's a new month with new goals! Are you going in a different direction or building on the work you did in month 1? Either way, you can rest easy knowing you're getting closer to the writer you want to be!

Monday Checklist:

☐ Writing _____

☐ Social media (15 min per 2-3 of following: Twit FB G+ LI Pin

☐ Promotion strategies/tactics

☐ Publishing progress post/article/book

☐ Other (in exchange for one of the above)

_____

Notes: _____

_____

_____

_____

_____

Tuesday Checklist:

☐ Writing _____

☐ Social media (15 min per 2-3 of following: Twit FB G+ LI Pin

☐ Promotion strategies/tactics

☐ Publishing progress post/article/book

☐ Other (in exchange for one of the above)

_____

Notes: _____

_____

_____

_____

_____

Wednesday Checklist:

☐Writing_____

☐ Social media (15 min per 2-3 of following: Twit FB G+ LI Pin

☐ Promotion strategies/tactics

☐ Publishing progress post/article/book

☐ Other (in exchange for one of the above)

Notes:_____
_____
_____
_____

Thursday Checklist:

☐Writing_____

☐ Social media (15 min per 2-3 of following: Twit FB G+ LI Pin

☐ Promotion strategies/tactics

☐ Publishing progress post/article/book

☐ Other (in exchange for one of the above)

Notes:_____
_____
_____
_____

Friday Checklist:

☐Writing_____

☐ Social media (15 min per 2-3 of following: Twit FB G+ LI Pin

☐ Promotion strategies/tactics

☐ Publishing progress post/article/book

☐ Other (in exchange for one of the above)

Notes:_____

_____

_____

_____

Saturday Checklist:

☐Writing_____

☐ Social media (15 min per 2-3 of following: Twit FB G+ LI Pin

☐ Promotion strategies/tactics

☐ Publishing progress post/article/book

☐ Other (in exchange for one of the above)

Notes:

_____

_____

_____

_____

Sunday-Funday!

Have you hiked every nearby trail? Visited your local library? Promise to do something like that and do *not* write today. The only thing you *might* do today is the below weekly assessment. You worked hard all week. You deserve a little fun!

Week 1 Goal Assessment:

☐ achieved
☐ partially achieved

If not completed, why?

_____

What can you change next week to achieve your goal? Or alternatively, if you achieved your goal, do you need to make any adjustments? If so, what?

_____

_____

_____

Week 2

This week's goal may need to be adjusted considering what you completed last week. You may have discovered you are an overachiever – or maybe you had a really difficult week because of things outside your control. Whatever the case, choose your goal accordingly. Always be gentle and realistic!

Week 2 Goal:

_____

_____

_____

Weekly thought:

You've established your routine. Your excitement about using your log is still high because now you're focused on a new monthly goal and you're seeing results. Keep working at it! You'll be amazed at how much you will accomplish!

Monday Checklist:

☐Writing_____

☐ Social media (15 min per 2-3 of following: Twit FB G+ LI Pin

☐ Promotion strategies/tactics

☐ Publishing progress post/article/book

☐ Other (in exchange for one of the above)

_____

Notes:_____

_____

_____

_____

_____

Tuesday Checklist:

☐Writing_____

☐ Social media (15 min per 2-3 of following: Twit FB G+ LI Pin

☐ Promotion strategies/tactics

☐ Publishing progress post/article/book

☐ Other (in exchange for one of the above)

_____

Notes:_____

_____

_____

_____

_____

Wednesday Checklist:

☐ Writing_____

☐ Social media (15 min per 2-3 of following: Twit FB G+ LI Pin

☐ Promotion strategies/tactics

☐ Publishing progress post/article/book

☐ Other (in exchange for one of the above)

Notes:_____
_____
_____
_____

Thursday Checklist:

☐ Writing_____

☐ Social media (15 min per 2-3 of following: Twit FB G+ LI Pin

☐ Promotion strategies/tactics

☐ Publishing progress post/article/book

☐ Other (in exchange for one of the above)

Notes:_____
_____
_____
_____

Friday Checklist:

☐ Writing _____

_____

☐ Social media (15 min per 2-3 of following: Twit FB G+ LI Pin

_____

☐ Promotion strategies/tactics

_____

☐ Publishing progress post/article/book

_____

☐ Other (in exchange for one of the above)

_____

Notes: _____

_____

_____

_____

Saturday Checklist:

☐ Writing _____

_____

☐ Social media (15 min per 2-3 of following: Twit FB G+ LI Pin

_____

☐ Promotion strategies/tactics

_____

☐ Publishing progress post/article/book

_____

☐ Other (in exchange for one of the above)

_____

Notes:

_____

_____

_____

_____

Sunday-Funday!

Take a break! The only thing you *might* do today is the below weekly assessment. You worked hard all week. You deserve a little fun!

Week 2 Goal Assessment:

☐ achieved
☐ partially achieved

If not completed, why?

_____

What can you change next week to achieve your goal? Or alternatively, if you achieved your goal, do you need to make any adjustments? If so, what?

_____
_____
_____

Week 3

By now you have probably had some really productive weeks and then others that were a struggle. The key is keeping a balance between the two. By training yourself to keep your goals in mind, you'll continue to make progress despite those inevitable setbacks. Ultimately, that's all you want – continued progress. Keep logging!

Week 3 Goal:

_____

_____

_____

Weekly thought:

Even when things get difficult, you have writer's block or you're not getting the reception you expected, the difference between successful and unsuccessful writers is persistence. Keep working. Stay focused. Setbacks are temporary. Accomplishments stay with you.

Monday Checklist:

☐ Writing_____

_____

☐ Social media (15 min per 2-3 of following: Twit FB G+ LI Pin

_____

☐ Promotion strategies/tactics

_____

☐ Publishing progress post/article/book

_____

☐ Other (in exchange for one of the above)

_____

Notes:_____

_____

_____

_____

_____

Tuesday Checklist:

☐ Writing_____

_____

☐ Social media (15 min per 2-3 of following: Twit FB G+ LI Pin

_____

☐ Promotion strategies/tactics

_____

☐ Publishing progress post/article/book

_____

☐ Other (in exchange for one of the above)

_____

Notes:_____

_____

_____

_____

_____

Wednesday Checklist:

☐ Writing_____

☐ Social media (15 min per 2-3 of following: Twit FB G+ LI Pin

☐ Promotion strategies/tactics

☐ Publishing progress post/article/book

☐ Other (in exchange for one of the above)

Notes:_____

_____

_____

Thursday Checklist:

☐ Writing_____

☐ Social media (15 min per 2-3 of following: Twit FB G+ LI Pin

☐ Promotion strategies/tactics

☐ Publishing progress post/article/book

☐ Other (in exchange for one of the above)

Notes:_____

_____

_____

Friday Checklist:

☐Writing_____

☐ Social media (15 min per 2-3 of following: Twit FB G+ LI Pin

☐ Promotion strategies/tactics

☐ Publishing progress post/article/book

☐ Other (in exchange for one of the above)

Notes:_____

_____

_____

_____

Saturday Checklist:

☐Writing_____

☐ Social media (15 min per 2-3 of following: Twit FB G+ LI Pin

☐ Promotion strategies/tactics

☐ Publishing progress post/article/book

☐ Other (in exchange for one of the above)

Notes:

_____

_____

_____

_____

Sunday-Funday!

Go easy today! The only thing you *might* do related to your goals is the below weekly assessment. You worked hard all week. You deserve a little fun!

Week 3 Goal Assessment:

☐ achieved
☐ partially achieved

If not completed, why?

_____

What can you change next week to achieve your goal? Or alternatively, if you achieved your goal, do you need to make any adjustments? If so, what?

_____

_____

_____

Week 4

You've done so much! Still, you don't want to lose focus. What is left to do to accomplish your monthly goals? Be sure to push as you need in order to reach them. You want to feel successful, but be careful you don't fry your brain (or motivation!) in the process!

Week 4 Goal:

_____

_____

_____

Weekly thought:

This is the last week in your monthly goal! At the end of this week, you'll be approximately 33% finished with your 6 month goal. That is so exciting! Every day you're doing more, getting better, and growing closer to where you want to be! Keep working and you'll get there!

Monday Checklist:

☐Writing_____

☐ Social media (15 min per 2-3 of following: Twit FB G+ LI Pin

☐ Promotion strategies/tactics

☐ Publishing progress post/article/book

☐ Other (in exchange for one of the above)

_____

Notes:_____

_____

_____

_____

Tuesday Checklist:

☐Writing_____

☐ Social media (15 min per 2-3 of following: Twit FB G+ LI Pin

☐ Promotion strategies/tactics

☐ Publishing progress post/article/book

☐ Other (in exchange for one of the above)

_____

Notes:_____

_____

_____

_____

Wednesday Checklist:

☐ Writing_____

☐ Social media (15 min per 2-3 of following: Twit FB G+ LI Pin

☐ Promotion strategies/tactics

☐ Publishing progress post/article/book

☐ Other (in exchange for one of the above)

Notes:_____
_____
_____
_____

Thursday Checklist:

☐ Writing_____

☐ Social media (15 min per 2-3 of following: Twit FB G+ LI Pin

☐ Promotion strategies/tactics

☐ Publishing progress post/article/book

☐ Other (in exchange for one of the above)

Notes:_____
_____
_____
_____

Friday Checklist:

☐Writing_____

_____

☐ Social media (15 min per 2-3 of following: Twit FB G+ LI Pin

_____

☐ Promotion strategies/tactics

_____

☐ Publishing progress post/article/book

_____

☐ Other (in exchange for one of the above)

_____

Notes:_____

_____

_____

Saturday Checklist:

☐Writing_____

_____

☐ Social media (15 min per 2-3 of following: Twit FB G+ LI Pin

_____

☐ Promotion strategies/tactics

_____

☐ Publishing progress post/article/book

_____

☐ Other (in exchange for one of the above)

_____

Notes:

_____

_____

_____

Sunday-Funday!

Have you checked out the local museums? Watched a home game of a local team? The only things you *might* do today are the weekly and monthly assessments. You worked hard all week. You deserve a little fun!

Week 4 Goal Assessment:

☐ achieved
☐ partially achieved

If not completed, why?

_____

What can you change next week to achieve your goal? Or alternatively, if you achieved your goal, do you need to make any adjustments? If so, what?

_____
_____
_____

Month 1 Goal Assessment:

☐ achieved
☐ partially achieved

If not completed, why?

_____

What can you change next week to achieve your goal? Or alternatively, if you achieved your goal, do you need to make any adjustments? If so, what?

_____
_____
_____

MONTH 3

Below write down your month 3 goals in the following areas as needed.

Writing:

_____

_____

Social media:

_____

_____

Promotion:

_____

_____

Publishing:

_____

_____

Other:

_____

_____

Monthly goal statement (written as though it is reality):

_____

_____

_____

_____

_____

_____

_____

Week 1

Take a few minutes now to portion out your monthly goal into weekly goals. If you intend to begin a manuscript (or are continuing one from the past two months), estimate how many words you need to complete the book and then divide it into manageable portions. If you were writing a novel, aiming for approximately 90,000 words would be reasonable. At 2000 words per day, that would mean you'd finish writing in 45 days. If you're editing a manuscript, I recommend a set page or chapter count per day.

Six days writing at 2000 words daily means your weekly goal would be 12,000 words. Alternatively, six days editing ten pages daily means at the end of the week you should have completed editing on 60 pages. It also means you know how much you have left to complete in week 2, and possibly week 3.

Week 1 Goal:

_____

_____

_____

Weekly thought:

Congratulations! You're nearing the half-way mark in your log! Now it is more important than ever to keep to a manageable pace. You don't want to burnout before you've reached your goals. Slow and steady is the key to accomplishment.

Monday Checklist:

□Writing _____

□ Social media (15 min per 2-3 of following: Twit FB G+ LI Pin

□ Promotion strategies/tactics

□ Publishing progress post/article/book

□ Other (in exchange for one of the above)

Notes:_____

_____

_____

_____

_____

Tuesday Checklist:

□Writing _____

□ Social media (15 min per 2-3 of following: Twit FB G+ LI Pin

□ Promotion strategies/tactics

□ Publishing progress post/article/book

□ Other (in exchange for one of the above)

Notes:_____

_____

_____

_____

_____

Wednesday Checklist:

☐Writing_____

☐ Social media (15 min per 2-3 of following: Twit FB G+ LI Pin

☐ Promotion strategies/tactics

☐ Publishing progress post/article/book

☐ Other (in exchange for one of the above)

Notes:_____
_____
_____
_____

Thursday Checklist:

☐Writing_____

☐ Social media (15 min per 2-3 of following: Twit FB G+ LI Pin

☐ Promotion strategies/tactics

☐ Publishing progress post/article/book

☐ Other (in exchange for one of the above)

Notes:_____
_____
_____
_____

Friday Checklist:

☐Writing_____

☐ Social media (15 min per 2-3 of following: Twit FB G+ LI Pin

☐ Promotion strategies/tactics

☐ Publishing progress post/article/book

☐ Other (in exchange for one of the above)

Notes:_____

_____

_____

_____

Saturday Checklist:

☐Writing_____

☐ Social media (15 min per 2-3 of following: Twit FB G+ LI Pin

☐ Promotion strategies/tactics

☐ Publishing progress post/article/book

☐ Other (in exchange for one of the above)

Notes:

_____

_____

_____

_____

Sunday-Funday!

Make a real effort to *not* write today. The only thing you *might* do today is the below weekly assessment. You worked hard all week. You deserve a little fun!

Week 1 Goal Assessment:

☐ achieved
☐ partially achieved

If not completed, why?

_____

What can you change next week to achieve your goal? Or alternatively, if you achieved your goal, do you need to make any adjustments? If so, what?

_____
_____
_____

Week 2

Adjust this week's goal depending on what you completed last week. If you were not able to keep up that 2000 word count pace, drop your daily count. If you struggled to edit 10 pages, drop it down to 5. Figure out what is sustainable for you. Forgive yourself if you weren't able to do as much as you thought. You may be a writer, but you're still human!

Week 2 Goal:

_____

_____

_____

Weekly thought:

You may be going into a little bit of a slump. It's been over two months since you began logging. Drum up excitement by looking back at what you've achieved. You *are* living your dream and that is inspiring in itself!

Monday Checklist:

☐ Writing _____

☐ Social media (15 min per 2-3 of following: Twit FB G+ LI Pin

☐ Promotion strategies/tactics

☐ Publishing progress post/article/book

☐ Other (in exchange for one of the above)

_____

Notes: _____

_____

_____

_____

_____

Tuesday Checklist:

☐ Writing _____

☐ Social media (15 min per 2-3 of following: Twit FB G+ LI Pin

☐ Promotion strategies/tactics

☐ Publishing progress post/article/book

☐ Other (in exchange for one of the above)

_____

Notes: _____

_____

_____

_____

_____

Wednesday Checklist:

☐Writing_____

☐ Social media (15 min per 2-3 of following: Twit FB G+ LI Pin

☐ Promotion strategies/tactics

☐ Publishing progress post/article/book

☐ Other (in exchange for one of the above)

Notes:_____
_____
_____
_____

Thursday Checklist:

☐Writing_____

☐ Social media (15 min per 2-3 of following: Twit FB G+ LI Pin

☐ Promotion strategies/tactics

☐ Publishing progress post/article/book

☐ Other (in exchange for one of the above)

Notes:_____
_____
_____
_____

Friday Checklist:

☐ Writing_____

☐ Social media (15 min per 2-3 of following: Twit FB G+ LI Pin

☐ Promotion strategies/tactics

☐ Publishing progress post/article/book

☐ Other (in exchange for one of the above)

Notes:_____
_____
_____

Saturday Checklist:

☐ Writing_____

☐ Social media (15 min per 2-3 of following: Twit FB G+ LI Pin

☐ Promotion strategies/tactics

☐ Publishing progress post/article/book

☐ Other (in exchange for one of the above)

Notes:

_____
_____
_____

Sunday-Funday!

Have you watched an entire movie series? You could start today if there's something you really want to see. The only thing you *might* do related to writing is the below weekly assessment. You worked hard all week. You deserve a little fun!

Week 2 Goal Assessment:

☐ achieved
☐ partially achieved

If not completed, why?

_____

What can you change next week to achieve your goal? Or alternatively, if you achieved your goal, do you need to make any adjustments? If so, what?

_____

_____

_____

Week 3

At this point you have quite a body of work. You may have discovered there are some things you hadn't thought of when you began this journey and you've had to revisit your long term goals. Maybe you've already surpassed your wildest dreams. If so, go bigger! What can't you do when you put your mind to it? What are your limits? The truth is, if you are committed, you will reach your goal. If you've made it thus far in the log, you have the level of commitment necessary to do great things with your writing.

Week 3 Goal:

_____

_____

_____

Weekly thought:

Keep in mind, sometimes when you achieve your goals, they look differently than you imagined. You may wake up one day and realize you've mastered writing through publishing a library of books in the span of five years. Maybe the books were different genres. Maybe you thought mastery would feel different. It's important to recognize when you achieve a goal, even if it isn't exactly _how_ you expected it to be. Let go of specifics and be willing to see things a different way. You'll be glad you did.

Monday Checklist:

☐ Writing_____

☐ Social media (15 min per 2-3 of following: Twit FB G+ LI Pin

☐ Promotion strategies/tactics

☐ Publishing progress post/article/book

☐ Other (in exchange for one of the above)

Notes:_____

_____

_____

_____

_____

Tuesday Checklist:

☐ Writing_____

☐ Social media (15 min per 2-3 of following: Twit FB G+ LI Pin

☐ Promotion strategies/tactics

☐ Publishing progress post/article/book

☐ Other (in exchange for one of the above)

Notes:_____

_____

_____

_____

_____

Wednesday Checklist

☐Writing_____

☐ Social media (15 min per 2-3 of following: Twit FB G+ LI Pin

☐ Promotion strategies/tactics

☐ Publishing progress post/article/book

☐ Other (in exchange for one of the above)

Notes:_____

_____

_____

_____

Thursday Checklist:

☐Writing_____

☐ Social media (15 min per 2-3 of following: Twit FB G+ LI Pin

☐ Promotion strategies/tactics

☐ Publishing progress post/article/book

☐ Other (in exchange for one of the above)

Notes:_____

_____

_____

_____

_____

Friday Checklist:

☐ Writing_____

☐ Social media (15 min per 2-3 of following: Twit FB G+ LI Pin

☐ Promotion strategies/tactics

☐ Publishing progress post/article/book

☐ Other (in exchange for one of the above)

Notes:_____

_____

_____

Saturday Checklist:

☐ Writing_____

☐ Social media (15 min per 2-3 of following: Twit FB G+ LI Pin

☐ Promotion strategies/tactics

☐ Publishing progress post/article/book

☐ Other (in exchange for one of the above)

Notes:

_____

_____

_____

Sunday-Funday!

Make a real effort to *not* write today. The only thing you *might* do today is the below weekly assessment. You worked hard all week. You deserve a little fun!

Week 3 Goal Assessment:

☐ achieved
☐ partially achieved

If not completed, why?

_____

What can you change next week to achieve your goal? Or alternatively, if you achieved your goal, do you need to make any adjustments? If so, what?

_____

_____

_____

Week 4

Keep your momentum. Adjust your pace and resources as needed to achieve this month's goals. Remember – at the end of this week you will have finished 3 months worth of work. That means you'll be half way to your six month goal!

Week 4 Goal:

_____

_____

_____

Weekly thought:

This is the last week in your monthly goal! At the end of this week, you'll be approximately 50% finished with your 6 month goal. Isn't that exciting? This is huge! Every day you're doing more, getting better, and growing closer to where you want to be! Keep working and you'll get there!

Monday Checklist:

☐ Writing_____

☐ Social media (15 min per 2-3 of following: Twit FB G+ LI Pin

☐ Promotion strategies/tactics

☐ Publishing progress post/article/book

☐ Other (in exchange for one of the above)

_____

Notes:_____

_____
_____
_____
_____

Tuesday Checklist:

☐ Writing_____

☐ Social media (15 min per 2-3 of following: Twit FB G+ LI Pin

☐ Promotion strategies/tactics

☐ Publishing progress post/article/book

☐ Other (in exchange for one of the above)

_____

Notes:_____

_____
_____
_____
_____

Wednesday Checklist

☐ Writing_____

☐ Social media (15 min per 2-3 of following: Twit FB G+ LI Pin

☐ Promotion strategies/tactics

☐ Publishing progress post/article/book

☐ Other (in exchange for one of the above)

Notes:_____

_____

_____

_____

Thursday Checklist:

☐ Writing_____

☐ Social media (15 min per 2-3 of following: Twit FB G+ LI Pin

☐ Promotion strategies/tactics

☐ Publishing progress post/article/book

☐ Other (in exchange for one of the above)

Notes:_____

_____

_____

_____

Friday Checklist:

☐Writing_____

☐ Social media (15 min per 2-3 of following: Twit FB G+ LI Pin

☐ Promotion strategies/tactics

☐ Publishing progress post/article/book

☐ Other (in exchange for one of the above)

Notes:_____

_____

_____

Saturday Checklist:

☐Writing_____

☐ Social media (15 min per 2-3 of following: Twit FB G+ LI Pin

☐ Promotion strategies/tactics

☐ Publishing progress post/article/book

☐ Other (in exchange for one of the above)

Notes:

_____

_____

_____

_____

Sunday-Funday!

Maybe get a haircut or a manicure. Or give yourself a home spa day. Or hang out in your underwear. Everyone needs a scheduled break. The only things you *might* do today are the weekly and monthly assessments. You worked hard all week. You deserve a little fun!

Week 4 Goal Assessment:

☐ achieved
☐ partially achieved

If not completed, why?

_____

What can you change next week to achieve your goal? Or alternatively, if you achieved your goal, do you need to make any adjustments? If so, what?

_____

_____

_____

Month 3 Goal Assessment

☐ achieved
☐ partially achieved

If not completed, why?

_____

What can you change next week to achieve your goal? Or alternatively, if you achieved your goal, do you need to make any adjustments? If so, what?

_____

_____

_____

MONTH 4

Below write down your month 4 goals in the following areas as needed.

Writing:

_____

_____

Social media:

_____

_____

Promotion:

_____

_____

Publishing:

_____

_____

Other:

_____

_____

Monthly goal statement (written as though it is reality):

_____

_____

_____

_____

_____

_____

_____

Week 1

Take a few minutes now to portion out your monthly goal into weekly goals. By this point in your 6 month process, you should be focusing on fine-tuning your work or tactics and strategies, depending on your goals. If something isn't working, spend your "other" goal connecting with experts or their material on the subject.

If you're like me, and struggled with marketing, then seek out experts, sign-up for newsletters, and make it a goal to read an hour daily on marketing until you feel you have enough information to formulate a plan of attack. Just because one thing didn't work, doesn't mean something else won't. Be patient and trust in the power of your commitment.

Week 1 Goal:

_____

_____

_____

Weekly thought:

If you haven't already, find a mentor or a writing group. It can meet in person or online. Writing is an isolating activity and it is good to have reminders that you are not alone in your pursuit. They can give you support when you're struggling or offer insights you couldn't reach on your own. Community makes writing richer and will help you achieve your goals.

Monday Checklist:

☐Writing_____

☐ Social media (15 min per 2-3 of following: Twit FB G+ LI Pin
_____

☐ Promotion strategies/tactics
_____

☐ Publishing progress post/article/book
_____

☐ Other (in exchange for one of the above)
_____

Notes:_____
_____
_____
_____
_____

Tuesday Checklist:

☐Writing_____

☐ Social media (15 min per 2-3 of following: Twit FB G+ LI Pin
_____

☐ Promotion strategies/tactics
_____

☐ Publishing progress post/article/book
_____

☐ Other (in exchange for one of the above)
_____

Notes:_____
_____
_____
_____
_____

Wednesday Checklist

- ☐ Writing_____
  _____

- ☐ Social media (15 min per 2-3 of following: Twit FB G+ LI Pin
  _____

- ☐ Promotion strategies/tactics
  _____

- ☐ Publishing progress post/article/book
  _____

- ☐ Other (in exchange for one of the above)
  _____

Notes:_____
_____
_____
_____

Thursday Checklist:

- ☐ Writing_____
  _____

- ☐ Social media (15 min per 2-3 of following: Twit FB G+ LI Pin

- ☐ Promotion strategies/tactics
  _____

- ☐ Publishing progress post/article/book
  _____

- ☐ Other (in exchange for one of the above)
  _____

Notes:_____
_____
_____
_____

Friday Checklist:

☐Writing_____

☐ Social media (15 min per 2-3 of following: Twit FB G+ LI Pin

☐ Promotion strategies/tactics

☐ Publishing progress post/article/book

☐ Other (in exchange for one of the above)

Notes:_____
_____
_____
_____

Saturday Checklist

☐Writing_____

☐ Social media (15 min per 2-3 of following: Twit FB G+ LI Pin

☐ Promotion strategies/tactics

☐ Publishing progress post/article/book

☐ Other (in exchange for one of the above)

Notes:
_____
_____
_____
_____

Sunday-Funday!

Sometimes it's good to do absolutely nothing. Make a real effort to *not* write today. The only thing you *might* do today is the below weekly assessment. You worked hard all week. You deserve a little fun!

Week 1 Goal Assessment:

☐ achieved
☐ partially achieved

If not completed, why?

_____

What can you change next week to achieve your goal? Or alternatively, if you achieved your goal, do you need to make any adjustments? If so, what?

_____
_____
_____

Week 2

Adjust this week's goal depending on what you completed last week. Keep what works, and cut out anything that doesn't. If you're finding yourself dragging or have lost motivation to work on a project, take a step back and do something else.

When I'm struggling with writing, I work on graphics. If that's giving me problems, I read about writing craft or small business strategy. And if nothing is happening, or I can't get myself to even work on small business pieces, I go for a walk or play with my toddler until I'm refreshed. It's okay if you need to work on something else related to writing. All work you do on writing moves you forward, but don't forget, you need to take care of yourself too. That is what allows you to reach your final goals.

Week 2 Goal:

_____
_____
_____

Weekly thought:

If you've lost momentum, work on something that excites you. Sometimes you have to change things up to maintain progress. Slow and steady is better than staying still!

Monday Checklist:

☐Writing_____

_____

☐ Social media (15 min per 2-3 of following: Twit FB G+ LI Pin

_____

☐ Promotion strategies/tactics

_____

☐ Publishing progress post/article/book

_____

☐ Other (in exchange for one of the above)

_____

Notes:_____

_____

_____

_____

_____

Tuesday Checklist:

☐Writing_____

_____

☐ Social media (15 min per 2-3 of following: Twit FB G+ LI Pin

_____

☐ Promotion strategies/tactics

_____

☐ Publishing progress post/article/book

_____

☐ Other (in exchange for one of the above)

_____

Notes:_____

_____

_____

_____

_____

Wednesday Checklist

☐ Writing_____

☐ Social media (15 min per 2-3 of following: Twit FB G+ LI Pin

☐ Promotion strategies/tactics

☐ Publishing progress post/article/book

☐ Other (in exchange for one of the above)

Notes:_____
_____
_____
_____

Thursday Checklist:

☐ Writing_____

☐ Social media (15 min per 2-3 of following: Twit FB G+ LI Pin

☐ Promotion strategies/tactics

☐ Publishing progress post/article/book

☐ Other (in exchange for one of the above)

Notes:_____
_____
_____
_____
_____

Friday Checklist:

☐ Writing_____

☐ Social media (15 min per 2-3 of following: Twit FB G+ LI Pin

☐ Promotion strategies/tactics

☐ Publishing progress post/article/book

☐ Other (in exchange for one of the above)

Notes:_____

_____

_____

_____

Saturday Checklist

☐ Writing_____

☐ Social media (15 min per 2-3 of following: Twit FB G+ LI Pin

☐ Promotion strategies/tactics

☐ Publishing progress post/article/book

☐ Other (in exchange for one of the above)

Notes:

_____

_____

_____

_____

Sunday-Funday!

I like going to free events and festivals. Are there any near you? The only thing writing related you *might* do today is the below weekly assessment. You worked hard all week. You deserve a little fun!

Week 2 Goal Assessment:

☐ achieved
☐ partially achieved

If not completed, why?

_____

What can you change next week to achieve your goal? Or alternatively, if you achieved your goal, do you need to make any adjustments? If so, what?

_____

_____

_____

Week 3

By this time, you know what you want to do with your writing. If you originally thought you were a hobbyist, maybe you've recognized you want more. If you originally thought you wanted to be a professional, maybe you recognize it's more work than you're willing to do. Either is fine if you accept this truth about you.

Week 3 Goal:

_____

_____

_____

Weekly thought:

When I first started writing, I thought I was being professional. I worked whenever the whim struck me, which meant I hardly ever wrote. I was unwilling to commit the time, energy, and resources necessary to really be a professional writer. Once I recognized my behavior, I was able to re-evaluate where I was as a writer and my calling. Through that, I reaffirmed my commitment to writing and developed the systems in this log. It helped me publish a library of books, create a website, and manage 3 blogs. I was able to see my weaknesses and determine routes to address them.

Affirm where you are and where you want to be. Recognize you're following the necessary steps to get there.

Monday Checklist:

☐Writing_____

☐ Social media (15 min per 2-3 of following: Twit FB G+ LI Pin

☐ Promotion strategies/tactics

☐ Publishing progress post/article/book

☐ Other (in exchange for one of the above)

Notes:_____

_____

_____

_____

Tuesday Checklist:

☐Writing_____

☐ Social media (15 min per 2-3 of following: Twit FB G+ LI Pin

☐ Promotion strategies/tactics

☐ Publishing progress post/article/book

☐ Other (in exchange for one of the above)

Notes:_____

_____

_____

_____

Wednesday Checklist

☐Writing_____

_____

☐ Social media (15 min per 2-3 of following: Twit FB G+ LI Pin

_____

☐ Promotion strategies/tactics

_____

☐ Publishing progress post/article/book

_____

☐ Other (in exchange for one of the above)

_____

Notes:_____

_____

_____

_____

Thursday Checklist:

☐Writing_____

_____

☐ Social media (15 min per 2-3 of following: Twit FB G+ LI Pin

_____

☐ Promotion strategies/tactics

_____

☐ Publishing progress post/article/book

_____

☐ Other (in exchange for one of the above)

_____

Notes:_____

_____

_____

_____

Friday Checklist:

☐Writing_____

☐ Social media (15 min per 2-3 of following: Twit FB G+ LI Pin

☐ Promotion strategies/tactics

☐ Publishing progress post/article/book

☐ Other (in exchange for one of the above)

Notes:_____

_____

_____

_____

Saturday Checklist:

☐Writing_____

☐ Social media (15 min per 2-3 of following: Twit FB G+ LI Pin

☐ Promotion strategies/tactics

☐ Publishing progress post/article/book

☐ Other (in exchange for one of the above)

Notes:

_____

_____

_____

_____

Sunday-Funday!

Everyone needs a scheduled break. The only thing you *might* do today is the below weekly assessment. You worked hard all week. You deserve a little fun!

Week 3 Goal Assessment:

☐ achieved
☐ partially achieved

If not completed, why?

_____

What can you change next week to achieve your goal? Or alternatively, if you achieved your goal, do you need to make any adjustments? If so, what?

_____
_____
_____

Week 4

Keep logging your progress every day. If you're struggling with logging immediately after you complete a task, just set aside a block of time to log before you go to sleep. That is also a good time to review the completed portions of your log. Whenever you start to lose motivation or struggle to maintain your progress, take a time to review everything you've accomplished in the past few months. It's quite remarkable to see your transformation through this process.

Week 4 Goal:

_____
_____
_____

Weekly thought:

This is the last week in your monthly goal! At the end of this week, you'll be approximately 66% finished with your 6 month goal. Isn't that exciting? This is a huge deal! Every day you're doing more, getting better, and growing closer to where you want to be! Keep working and you'll get there!

Monday Checklist:

☐ Writing _____

☐ Social media (15 min per 2-3 of following: Twit FB G+ LI Pin

☐ Promotion strategies/tactics

☐ Publishing progress post/article/book

☐ Other (in exchange for one of the above)

_____

Notes: _____

_____

_____

_____

_____

Tuesday Checklist:

☐ Writing _____

☐ Social media (15 min per 2-3 of following: Twit FB G+ LI Pin

☐ Promotion strategies/tactics

☐ Publishing progress post/article/book

☐ Other (in exchange for one of the above)

_____

Notes: _____

_____

_____

_____

_____

Wednesday Checklist

☐Writing_____

☐ Social media (15 min per 2-3 of following: Twit FB G+ LI Pin
_____

☐ Promotion strategies/tactics
_____

☐ Publishing progress post/article/book
_____

☐ Other (in exchange for one of the above)
_____

Notes:_____
_____
_____
_____

Thursday Checklist:

☐Writing_____

☐ Social media (15 min per 2-3 of following: Twit FB G+ LI Pin
_____

☐ Promotion strategies/tactics
_____

☐ Publishing progress post/article/book
_____

☐ Other (in exchange for one of the above)
_____

Notes:_____
_____
_____
_____

Friday Checklist:

☐ Writing _____

☐ Social media (15 min per 2-3 of following: Twit FB G+ LI Pin

☐ Promotion strategies/tactics

☐ Publishing progress post/article/book

☐ Other (in exchange for one of the above)

Notes: _____

_____

_____

Saturday Checklist:

☐ Writing _____

☐ Social media (15 min per 2-3 of following: Twit FB G+ LI Pin

☐ Promotion strategies/tactics

☐ Publishing progress post/article/book

☐ Other (in exchange for one of the above)

Notes:

_____

_____

_____

Sunday-Funday!

Ever made cheese? Picked fruit at an orchard? Just make an effort to *not* write today. The only things you *might* do today are the weekly and monthly assessments. You worked hard all week. You deserve a little fun!

Week 4 Goal Assessment:

☐ achieved
☐ partially achieved

If not completed, why?

_____

What can you change next week to achieve your goal? Or alternatively, if you achieved your goal, do you need to make any adjustments? If so, what?

_____

_____

_____

Month 4 Goal Assessment

☐ achieved
☐ partially achieved

If not completed, why?

_____

What can you change next week to achieve your goal? Or alternatively, if you achieved your goal, do you need to make any adjustments? If so, what?

_____

_____

_____

MONTH 5

Below write down your month 5 goals in the following areas as needed.

Writing:

_____

_____

Social media:

_____

_____

Promotion:

_____

_____

Publishing:

_____

_____

Other:

_____

_____

Monthly goal statement (written as though it is reality):

_____

_____

_____

_____

_____

_____

_____

Week 1

Take a few minutes now to portion out your monthly goal into weekly goals. If you're shopping a manuscript to agents or short stories and articles to magazines, you may be experiencing some dejection. You cannot control how your work is received, only what you do.

If you have been successful getting your work published – congratulations! If not, use rejected submissions as a jumping off point for your goals. Spend time reworking, re-reading. Invest in editorial services. Ask for feedback. Revisit your database of agents or magazines. There are always more places to submit your work. Sometimes it is just a matter of finding the right home for your work.

Week 1 Goal:

_____

_____

_____

Weekly thought:

Rejection is never about you, but about the agent or magazine. Just because your work gets rejected does not mean you should stop. If anything, it means you should keep going. This is the difference between the committed writer and everyone else. Every professional writer has experienced rejection. It is part of the process. Relish your connection to the scores of best-selling authors who have been rejected by agents, publishers, and magazines. You've joined their club!

Monday Checklist:

☐Writing_____

☐ Social media (15 min per 2-3 of following: Twit FB G+ LI Pin

☐ Promotion strategies/tactics

☐ Publishing progress post/article/book

☐ Other (in exchange for one of the above)

Notes:_____
_____
_____
_____
_____

Tuesday Checklist:

☐Writing_____

☐ Social media (15 min per 2-3 of following: Twit FB G+ LI Pin

☐ Promotion strategies/tactics

☐ Publishing progress post/article/book

☐ Other (in exchange for one of the above)

Notes:_____
_____
_____
_____
_____

Wednesday Checklist

☐Writing_____

☐ Social media (15 min per 2-3 of following: Twit FB G+ LI Pin

☐ Promotion strategies/tactics

☐ Publishing progress post/article/book

☐ Other (in exchange for one of the above)

Notes:_____

_____

_____

_____

Thursday Checklist:

☐Writing_____

☐ Social media (15 min per 2-3 of following: Twit FB G+ LI Pin

☐ Promotion strategies/tactics

☐ Publishing progress post/article/book

☐ Other (in exchange for one of the above)

Notes:_____

_____

_____

_____

Friday Checklist:

☐ Writing_____

☐ Social media (15 min per 2-3 of following: Twit FB G+ LI Pin

☐ Promotion strategies/tactics

☐ Publishing progress post/article/book

☐ Other (in exchange for one of the above)

Notes:_____

_____

_____

Saturday Checklist

☐ Writing_____

☐ Social media (15 min per 2-3 of following: Twit FB G+ LI Pin

☐ Promotion strategies/tactics

☐ Publishing progress post/article/book

☐ Other (in exchange for one of the above)

Notes:

_____

_____

_____

Sunday-Funday!

Is there a local theater company? The only thing related to writing you *might* do today is the below weekly assessment. You worked hard all week. You deserve a little fun!

Week 1 Goal Assessment:

☐ achieved
☐ partially achieved

If not completed, why?

_____

What can you change next week to achieve your goal? Or alternatively, if you achieved your goal, do you need to make any adjustments? If so, what?

_____
_____
_____

Week 2

t our daily count. If you struggled to edit 10 pages, drop it down to 5. Figure out what is sustainable for you. Forgive yourself if you weren't able to do as much as you thought. You may be a writer, but you're still human!

Week 2 Goal:

_____

_____

_____

Weekly thought:

You may be going into a little bit of a slump. It's been over two months since you began logging. Drum up excitement by looking back at what you've achieved. You *are* living your dream and that is inspiring in itself!

Monday Checklist:

☐ Writing_____

☐ Social media (15 min per 2-3 of following: Twit FB G+ LI Pin
_____

☐ Promotion strategies/tactics
_____

☐ Publishing progress post/article/book
_____

☐ Other (in exchange for one of the above)
_____

Notes:_____
_____
_____
_____
_____

Tuesday Checklist:

☐ Writing_____

☐ Social media (15 min per 2-3 of following: Twit FB G+ LI Pin
_____

☐ Promotion strategies/tactics
_____

☐ Publishing progress post/article/book
_____

☐ Other (in exchange for one of the above)
_____

Notes:_____
_____
_____
_____
_____

Wednesday Checklist

☐Writing_____

☐ Social media (15 min per 2-3 of following: Twit FB G+ LI Pin
_____

☐ Promotion strategies/tactics
_____

☐ Publishing progress post/article/book
_____

☐ Other (in exchange for one of the above)
_____

Notes:_____
_____
_____
_____

Thursday Checklist:

☐Writing_____

☐ Social media (15 min per 2-3 of following: Twit FB G+ LI Pin
_____

☐ Promotion strategies/tactics
_____

☐ Publishing progress post/article/book
_____

☐ Other (in exchange for one of the above)
_____

Notes:_____
_____
_____
_____

Friday Checklist:

☐ Writing_____

☐ Social media (15 min per 2-3 of following: Twit FB G+ LI Pin

☐ Promotion strategies/tactics

☐ Publishing progress post/article/book

☐ Other (in exchange for one of the above)

Notes:_____

_____

_____

Saturday Checklist

☐ Writing_____

☐ Social media (15 min per 2-3 of following: Twit FB G+ LI Pin

☐ Promotion strategies/tactics

☐ Publishing progress post/article/book

☐ Other (in exchange for one of the above)

Notes:

_____

_____

_____

Sunday-Funday!

Schedule a get-together with friends. Everyone needs a scheduled break. The only thing you *might* do today is the below weekly assessment. You worked hard all week. You deserve a little fun!

Week 2 Goal Assessment:

☐ achieved
☐ partially achieved

If not completed, why?

_____

What can you change next week to achieve your goal? Or alternatively, if you achieved your goal, do you need to make any adjustments? If so, what?

_____
_____
_____

Week 3

At this point you have quite a body of work. You may have discovered there are some things you hadn't thought of when you began this journey and you've had to revisit your long term goals. Maybe you've already surpassed your wildest dreams. If so, go bigger! What can't you do when you put your mind to it? What are your limits? The truth is, if you are committed, you will reach your goal. If you've made it thus far in the log, you have the level of commitment necessary to do great things with your writing.

Week 3 Goal:

_____

_____

_____

Weekly thought:

Keep in mind, sometimes when you achieve your goals, they look differently than you imagined. You may wake up one day and realize you've mastered writing through publishing a library of books in the span of five years. Maybe the books were different genres. Maybe you thought mastery would feel different. It's important to recognize when you achieve a goal, even if it isn't exactly _how_ you expected it to be. Let go of specifics and be willing to see things a different way. You'll be glad you did.

Monday Checklist:

☐Writing_____

_____

☐ Social media (15 min per 2-3 of following: Twit FB G+ LI Pin

_____

☐ Promotion strategies/tactics

_____

☐ Publishing progress post/article/book

_____

☐ Other (in exchange for one of the above)

_____

Notes:_____

_____

_____

_____

_____

Tuesday Checklist:

☐Writing_____

_____

☐ Social media (15 min per 2-3 of following: Twit FB G+ LI Pin

_____

☐ Promotion strategies/tactics

_____

☐ Publishing progress post/article/book

_____

☐ Other (in exchange for one of the above)

_____

Notes:_____

_____

_____

_____

_____

Wednesday Checklist

☐ Writing_____

☐ Social media (15 min per 2-3 of following: Twit FB G+ LI Pin

☐ Promotion strategies/tactics

☐ Publishing progress post/article/book

☐ Other (in exchange for one of the above)

Notes:_____

_____

_____

_____

Thursday Checklist:

☐ Writing_____

☐ Social media (15 min per 2-3 of following: Twit FB G+ LI Pin

☐ Promotion strategies/tactics

☐ Publishing progress post/article/book

☐ Other (in exchange for one of the above)

Notes:_____

_____

_____

_____

Friday Checklist:

☐ Writing _____

☐ Social media (15 min per 2-3 of following: Twit FB G+ LI Pin

☐ Promotion strategies/tactics

☐ Publishing progress post/article/book

☐ Other (in exchange for one of the above)

Notes: _____

_____

_____

_____

Saturday Checklist:

☐ Writing _____

☐ Social media (15 min per 2-3 of following: Twit FB G+ LI Pin

☐ Promotion strategies/tactics

☐ Publishing progress post/article/book

☐ Other (in exchange for one of the above)

Notes:

_____

_____

_____

_____

Sunday-Funday!

Everyone needs a scheduled break. Go lounge in a nearby cafe and watch the interesting people. The only thing related to writing you *might* do today is the below weekly assessment. You worked hard all week. You deserve a little fun!

Week 3 Goal Assessment:

☐ achieved
☐ partially achieved

If not completed, why?

_____

What can you change next week to achieve your goal? Or alternatively, if you achieved your goal, do you need to make any adjustments? If so, what?

_____
_____
_____

Week 4

Keep your momentum. Adjust your pace and resources as needed to achieve this month's goals. Remember – at the end of this week you will have finished 3 months worth of work. That means you'll be half way to your six month goal!

Week 4 Goal:

_____
_____
_____

Weekly thought:

This is the last week in your monthly goal! At the end of this week, you'll be approximately 83% finished with your 6 month goal. Isn't that exciting? This is huge! Every day you're doing more, getting better, and growing closer to where you want to be! Keep working and you'll get there!

Monday Checklist:

☐ Writing_____

☐ Social media (15 min per 2-3 of following: Twit FB G+ LI Pin

☐ Promotion strategies/tactics

☐ Publishing progress post/article/book

☐ Other (in exchange for one of the above)

Notes:_____
_____
_____
_____
_____

Tuesday Checklist:

☐ Writing_____

☐ Social media (15 min per 2-3 of following: Twit FB G+ LI Pin

☐ Promotion strategies/tactics

☐ Publishing progress post/article/book

☐ Other (in exchange for one of the above) .

Notes:_____
_____
_____
_____
_____

Wednesday Checklist

☐Writing_____

☐ Social media (15 min per 2-3 of following: Twit FB G+ Ll Pin

☐ Promotion strategies/tactics

☐ Publishing progress post/article/book

☐ Other (in exchange for one of the above)

Notes:_____

_____

_____

Thursday Checklist:

☐Writing_____

☐ Social media (15 min per 2-3 of following: Twit FB G+ Ll Pin

☐ Promotion strategies/tactics

☐ Publishing progress post/article/book

☐ Other (in exchange for one of the above)

Notes:_____

_____

_____

_____

Friday Checklist:

☐Writing_____

☐ Social media (15 min per 2-3 of following: Twit FB G+ LI Pin

☐ Promotion strategies/tactics

☐ Publishing progress post/article/book

☐ Other (in exchange for one of the above)

Notes:_____
_____
_____
_____

Saturday Checklist:

☐Writing_____

☐ Social media (15 min per 2-3 of following: Twit FB G+ LI Pin

☐ Promotion strategies/tactics

☐ Publishing progress post/article/book

☐ Other (in exchange for one of the above)

Notes:
_____
_____
_____
_____

Sunday-Funday!

I don't care if you're behind. Everyone needs a scheduled break. Do *not* write today. The only things you *might* do today are the weekly and monthly assessments. You worked hard all week. You deserve a little fun!

Week 4 Goal Assessment:

☐ achieved
☐ partially achieved

If not completed, why?

_____

What can you change next week to achieve your goal? Or alternatively, if you achieved your goal, do you need to make any adjustments? If so, what?

_____

_____

_____

Month 5 Goal Assessment

☐ achieved
☐ partially achieved

If not completed, why?

_____

What can you change next week to achieve your goal? Or alternatively, if you achieved your goal, do you need to make any adjustments? If so, what?

_____

_____

_____

MONTH 6

Below write down your month 6 goals in the following areas as needed.

Writing:

_____

_____

Social media:

_____

_____

Promotion:

_____

_____

Publishing:

_____

_____

Other:

_____

_____

Monthly goal statement (written as though it is reality):

_____

_____

_____

_____

_____

_____

Week 1

Because this is the last month, you want to review your six month goal and see how much you have remaining to achieve. It may be that your original goal was unrealistic (for example, publishing 10 short stories when you had never written one!). Or maybe you low-balled and have already achieved it. Now is the time to review and adjust accordingly.

If you have some work to do in order to reach your goals, pick up your pace. Recruit family and friends to help out with tasks like research, social media sharing, or promotion. When they see your commitment, you'll be surprised how willing they are to contribute to your cause!.

Week 1 Goal:

_____

_____

_____

Weekly thought:

Now is the last leg in your marathon. Be sure to finish strong. If you need to, review your monthly or original six month goal *every night* before bed or *every morning* when you wake. Feel what it feels like to have that goal accomplished. See it in your mind's eye. Doesn't it feel good? Of course it does! Now make it happen!

Monday Checklist:

☐ Writing _____

☐ Social media (15 min per 2-3 of following: Twit FB G+ LI Pin

☐ Promotion strategies/tactics

☐ Publishing progress post/article/book

☐ Other (in exchange for one of the above)

_____

Notes: _____

_____
_____
_____
_____

Tuesday Checklist:

☐ Writing _____

☐ Social media (15 min per 2-3 of following: Twit FB G+ LI Pin

☐ Promotion strategies/tactics

☐ Publishing progress post/article/book

☐ Other (in exchange for one of the above)

_____

Notes: _____

_____
_____
_____
_____

Wednesday Checklist

☐Writing_____

☐ Social media (15 min per 2-3 of following: Twit FB G+ LI Pin

☐ Promotion strategies/tactics

☐ Publishing progress post/article/book

☐ Other (in exchange for one of the above)

Notes:_____
_____
_____
_____

Thursday Checklist:

☐Writing_____

☐ Social media (15 min per 2-3 of following: Twit FB G+ LI Pin

☐ Promotion strategies/tactics

☐ Publishing progress post/article/book

☐ Other (in exchange for one of the above)

Notes:_____
_____
_____
_____

Friday Checklist:

☐ Writing_____

☐ Social media (15 min per 2-3 of following: Twit FB G+ LI Pin

☐ Promotion strategies/tactics

☐ Publishing progress post/article/book

☐ Other (in exchange for one of the above)

Notes:_____

Saturday Checklist

☐ Writing_____

☐ Social media (15 min per 2-3 of following: Twit FB G+ LI Pin

☐ Promotion strategies/tactics

☐ Publishing progress post/article/book

☐ Other (in exchange for one of the above)

Notes:

Sunday-Funday!

Everyone needs a scheduled break - even during crunch time. The only thing for today is the below weekly assessment. You worked hard all week. You deserve a little fun!

Week 1 Goal Assessment:

☐ achieved
☐ partially achieved

If not completed, why?

_____

What can you change next week to achieve your goal? Or alternatively, if you achieved your goal, do you need to make any adjustments? If so, what?

_____
_____
_____

Week 2

Adjust this week's goal depending on what you completed last week. Remember you only have two more weeks after this. Now is the time to push (within reason!). Put your power tunes on your stereo or get your earplugs – whatever you need to maintain your focus. Find every spare moment and minute to get that last bit of editing, submission, reading, or writing.

In the past, I've found it helpful to write down my entire schedule the night before so there is no question about what I'm doing at any given moment of my day. However if you have a lot of obligations and responsibilities (like kids), that might be impossible. In that case, seize every spare moment. Try to make it as seamless as possible by having everything necessary mobile and at your fingertips.

Week 2 Goal:

_____

_____

_____

Weekly thought:

This is your time. If you're working on a bucket list item or writing is your passion, do not let a hyperactive child or a nay-saying acquaintance get in your way. This is your moment – take it! Nothing was accomplished by giving up.

Monday Checklist:

- [ ] Writing_____

- [ ] Social media (15 min per 2-3 of following: Twit FB G+ LI Pin

- [ ] Promotion strategies/tactics

- [ ] Publishing progress post/article/book

- [ ] Other (in exchange for one of the above)

Notes:_____
_____
_____
_____
_____

Tuesday Checklist:

- [ ] Writing_____

- [ ] Social media (15 min per 2-3 of following: Twit FB G+ LI Pin

- [ ] Promotion strategies/tactics

- [ ] Publishing progress post/article/book

- [ ] Other (in exchange for one of the above)

Notes:_____
_____
_____
_____
_____

Wednesday Checklist

☐Writing_____

☐ Social media (15 min per 2-3 of following: Twit FB G+ LI Pin

☐ Promotion strategies/tactics

☐ Publishing progress post/article/book

☐ Other (in exchange for one of the above)

Notes:_____
_____
_____
_____

Thursday Checklist:

☐Writing_____

☐ Social media (15 min per 2-3 of following: Twit FB G+ LI Pin

☐ Promotion strategies/tactics

☐ Publishing progress post/article/book

☐ Other (in exchange for one of the above)

Notes:_____
_____
_____
_____

Friday Checklist:

☐Writing_____

☐ Social media (15 min per 2-3 of following: Twit FB G+ LI Pin

☐ Promotion strategies/tactics

☐ Publishing progress post/article/book

☐ Other (in exchange for one of the above)

_____

Notes:_____

_____

_____

_____

Saturday Checklist

☐Writing_____

☐ Social media (15 min per 2-3 of following: Twit FB G+ LI Pin

☐ Promotion strategies/tactics

☐ Publishing progress post/article/book

☐ Other (in exchange for one of the above)

_____

Notes:

_____

_____

_____

_____

Sunday-Funday!

Relax. You need to recharge. The only thing you *might* do today is the below weekly assessment. You worked hard all week. You deserve a little fun!

Week 2 Goal Assessment:

☐ achieved
☐ partially achieved

If not completed, why?

_____

What can you change next week to achieve your goal? Or alternatively, if you achieved your goal, do you need to make any adjustments? If so, what?

_____
_____
_____

Week 3

Hopefully now you're in the heat of content pushing – for a new blog, a completed manuscript, or a body of articles or short stories. Your writing goal has been supplanted by your "other" goal. This means you should be spending most of your time on promotion, social media, publishing, and honing your skill set. Reinforce your strengths and build up your weaknesses. Incorporate helpful feedback from mentors and colleagues. You have just two more weeks before you're finished. Keep pushing. You're almost there!

Week 3 Goal:

_____

_____

_____

Weekly thought:

Whatever direction your writing took over the last few months, it looks nothing like it did at the beginning. Take pride in this as you continue pushing towards your goal. You have done more than most ever dream of and that is remarkable!

Monday Checklist:

☐Writing_____

☐ Social media (15 min per 2-3 of following: Twit FB G+ LI Pin

☐ Promotion strategies/tactics

☐ Publishing progress post/article/book

☐ Other (in exchange for one of the above)

_____

Notes:_____

_____

_____

_____

_____

Tuesday Checklist:

☐Writing_____

☐ Social media (15 min per 2-3 of following: Twit FB G+ LI Pin

☐ Promotion strategies/tactics

☐ Publishing progress post/article/book

☐ Other (in exchange for one of the above)

_____

Notes:_____

_____

_____

_____

_____

Wednesday Checklist

☐Writing _____

☐ Social media (15 min per 2-3 of following: Twit FB G+ LI Pin

☐ Promotion strategies/tactics

☐ Publishing progress post/article/book

☐ Other (in exchange for one of the above)

Notes: _____

_____

_____

Thursday Checklist:

☐Writing _____

☐ Social media (15 min per 2-3 of following: Twit FB G+ LI Pin

☐ Promotion strategies/tactics

☐ Publishing progress post/article/book

☐ Other (in exchange for one of the above)

Notes: _____

_____

_____

_____

Friday Checklist:

- ☐ Writing_____

- ☐ Social media (15 min per 2-3 of following: Twit FB G+ LI Pin

- ☐ Promotion strategies/tactics

- ☐ Publishing progress post/article/book

- ☐ Other (in exchange for one of the above)

Notes:_____
_____
_____
_____

Saturday Checklist:

- ☐ Writing_____

- ☐ Social media (15 min per 2-3 of following: Twit FB G+ LI Pin

- ☐ Promotion strategies/tactics

- ☐ Publishing progress post/article/book

- ☐ Other (in exchange for one of the above)

Notes:

_____
_____
_____
_____

Sunday-Funday!

You're almost finished, but that doesn't mean you shouldn't have a break! The only thing you *might* do today is the below weekly assessment. You worked hard all week. You deserve a little fun!

Week 3 Goal Assessment:

☐ achieved
☐ partially achieved

If not completed, why?

_____

What can you change next week to achieve your goal? Or alternatively, if you achieved your goal, do you need to make any adjustments? If so, what?

_____
_____
_____

Week 4

Keep up your momentum! This is the LAST WEEK! Your tasks should be focused on tying up loose ends and polishing final tasks to achieve your goals. Keep your eye on your final goal. Read your goal statement aloud every night or every morning to keep it in mind. You're almost done. Finish strong!

Week 4 Goal:

_____

_____

_____

Weekly thought:

This is the last week in your big 6 month goal! At the end of this week, you'll be finished! Isn't that exciting? This is huge! Every day you're doing more, getting better, and growing closer to where you want to be! Keep working! You're almost there!

Monday Checklist:

☐Writing_____

☐ Social media (15 min per 2-3 of following: Twit FB G+ LI Pin

☐ Promotion strategies/tactics

☐ Publishing progress post/article/book

☐ Other (in exchange for one of the above)
_____

Notes:_____
_____
_____
_____
_____

Tuesday Checklist:

☐Writing_____

☐ Social media (15 min per 2-3 of following: Twit FB G+ LI Pin

☐ Promotion strategies/tactics

☐ Publishing progress post/article/book

☐ Other (in exchange for one of the above)
_____

Notes:_____
_____
_____
_____
_____

Wednesday Checklist

☐Writing_____

☐ Social media (15 min per 2-3 of following: Twit FB G+ LI Pin

☐ Promotion strategies/tactics

☐ Publishing progress post/article/book

☐ Other (in exchange for one of the above)

Notes:_____

_____

_____

Thursday Checklist:

☐Writing_____

☐ Social media (15 min per 2-3 of following: Twit FB G+ LI Pin

☐ Promotion strategies/tactics

☐ Publishing progress post/article/book

☐ Other (in exchange for one of the above)

Notes:_____

_____

_____

_____

Friday Checklist:

☐Writing_____

☐ Social media (15 min per 2-3 of following: Twit FB G+ LI Pin

☐ Promotion strategies/tactics

☐ Publishing progress post/article/book

☐ Other (in exchange for one of the above)

Notes:_____

Saturday Checklist:

☐Writing_____

☐ Social media (15 min per 2-3 of following: Twit FB G+ LI Pin

☐ Promotion strategies/tactics

☐ Publishing progress post/article/book

☐ Other (in exchange for one of the above)

Notes:

Sunday-Funday!

Breathe and do *nothing*. The only things you *might* do today are the weekly and monthly assessments. You worked hard all week. You deserve a little fun!

Week 4 Goal Assessment:

☐ achieved
☐ partially achieved

If not completed, why?

_____

What would you change to achieve your goal? Or alternatively, if you achieved your goal, how does it feel?

_____
_____
_____

Month 6 Goal Assessment

☐ achieved
☐ partially achieved

If not completed, why?

_____

What would you have changed to achieve your goal? Or alternatively, if you achieved your goal, how does it feel?

_____
_____
_____

THE 2 WEEK RESPITE

Congratulations! You finished your goal! You've earned a couple weeks to take it easy. That said, over the past few months, not only have you been working towards a set of goals, but you've also been building a routine or set of habits.

Habits require maintenance.

This means for the next couple weeks, while you're not working on a specific long term goal, you want to maintain a consistent work flow. This is especially important if you are a professional writer or if you have begun a blog with a regular readership.

With this in mind, I have included a more relaxed log for two weeks, after which, you may choose to begin a new log book in order to complete a new six month goal (remember the exercise in the goal-setting section at the beginning of this book?). This is the best way to continue progress on your "5 Year Plan" and maintain the new writing habits you've developed.

Some suggestions for how to spend your time in the next few weeks are:

- Evaluate where you are compared to where you want to be.
- Continue developing content for a website or blog
- Continue pushing content you have to magazines, agents, publishers etc.
- Revamp a media kit.
- Enroll in an e-course to improve or establish a skill set.
- Journal.
- Pick a few writing prompts.
- Schedule a photo shoot (for blog content, cover art, or head shots)

Respite Week 1

Congratulations! You did what few have done. Celebrate, but don't forget to maintain your writing habits. To do that, take a little time to decide what you'd like to do for the next couple weeks. Some things, like regular social media posting, are obvious. Others, like what you should write, may not be. Whatever you choose to work on, take it easy. This should be like a vacation.

Respite Week 1 Goal:

_____

_____

_____

Weekly thought:

Be sure to do something or visit somewhere this week that inspires you. After doing all that work, it's good to spend time nourishing that place in you that allows you to do all your creative work. Savor this break. You deserve it.

Monday Checklist:

☐ Writing _____

☐ Social media (15 min per 2-3 of following: Twit FB G+ LI Pin

☐ Promotion strategies/tactics

☐ Publishing progress post/article/book

☐ Other (in exchange for one of the above)

Notes:_____

_____

_____

_____

Tuesday Checklist:

☐ Writing _____

☐ Social media (15 min per 2-3 of following: Twit FB G+ LI Pin

☐ Promotion strategies/tactics

☐ Publishing progress post/article/book

☐ Other (in exchange for one of the above)

Notes:_____

_____

_____

_____

Wednesday Checklist

☐Writing_____

_____

☐ Social media (15 min per 2-3 of following: Twit FB G+ LI Pin

_____

☐ Promotion strategies/tactics

_____

☐ Publishing progress post/article/book

_____

☐ Other (in exchange for one of the above)

_____

Notes:_____

_____

_____

_____

Thursday Checklist:

☐Writing_____

_____

☐ Social media (15 min per 2-3 of following: Twit FB G+ LI Pin

_____

☐ Promotion strategies/tactics

_____

☐ Publishing progress post/article/book

_____

☐ Other (in exchange for one of the above)

_____

Notes:_____

_____

_____

_____

_____

Friday Checklist:

☐Writing_____

☐ Social media (15 min per 2-3 of following: Twit FB G+ LI Pin

☐ Promotion strategies/tactics

☐ Publishing progress post/article/book

☐ Other (in exchange for one of the above)

Notes:_____

_____

_____

_____

Saturday Checklist

☐Writing_____

☐ Social media (15 min per 2-3 of following: Twit FB G+ LI Pin

☐ Promotion strategies/tactics

☐ Publishing progress post/article/book

☐ Other (in exchange for one of the above)

Notes:

_____

_____

_____

_____

Sunday-Funday!

Watch a movie. Go swimming. Read a book. Go out with friends. Play a game. Watch a game. Go for a hike. Whatever you do today, make sure it has NOTHING to do with writing (except maybe the assessment below).

Respite Week 1 Goal Assessment:

☐ maintenance goal achieved
☐ maintenance goal partially achieved

Did you take a break this week? If not, why?

_____

Was it hard to cut down your pace or was it a welcome relief? What could you do to make it easier to slow down? Or, if you had an easy time, what made it easy to do?

_____
_____
_____
_____
_____
_____
_____
_____

Respite Week 2

This week should be spent doing two things: maintain writing habits and re-evaluating your next 6 month goal. If you plan to use a log like this again, make sure you have all your materials ready to go (and use expedited shipping if you're ordering online!).

If you're using *The Essential Author Log* a second time, spend at least one day of this week working through the 6 monthly goal exercise at the beginning of the book. You can take the second six month long term goal you established in this book. Or, alternatively, if you're finishing a year's work, you can go through the process for the second year of your five year plan.

It all depends on what you want to accomplish. Do what works best for you.

Respite Week 2 Goal:

_____

_____

_____

Weekly thought:

Relish the last bit of respite and lay the foundation for your next 6 months. You are a powerhouse and you have transformed yourself in such a short time. I am so proud of everything you've accomplished and I hope you are too.!

Monday Checklist:

☐Writing_____

☐ Social media (15 min per 2-3 of following: Twit FB G+ LI Pin

☐ Promotion strategies/tactics

☐ Publishing progress post/article/book

☐ Other (in exchange for one of the above)

Notes:_____
_____
_____
_____
_____

Tuesday Checklist:

☐Writing_____

☐ Social media (15 min per 2-3 of following: Twit FB G+ LI Pin

☐ Promotion strategies/tactics

☐ Publishing progress post/article/book

☐ Other (in exchange for one of the above)

Notes:_____
_____
_____
_____
_____

Wednesday Checklist

☐Writing_____

_____

☐ Social media (15 min per 2-3 of following: Twit FB G+ LI Pin

_____

☐ Promotion strategies/tactics

_____

☐ Publishing progress post/article/book

_____

☐ Other (in exchange for one of the above)

_____

Notes:_____

_____

_____

_____

Thursday Checklist:

☐Writing_____

_____

☐ Social media (15 min per 2-3 of following: Twit FB G+ LI Pin

_____

☐ Promotion strategies/tactics

_____

☐ Publishing progress post/article/book

_____

☐ Other (in exchange for one of the above)

_____

Notes:_____

_____

_____

_____

Friday Checklist:

☐Writing_____

☐ Social media (15 min per 2-3 of following: Twit FB G+ LI Pin

☐ Promotion strategies/tactics

☐ Publishing progress post/article/book

☐ Other (in exchange for one of the above)

Notes:_____

_____

_____

Saturday Checklist

☐Writing_____

☐ Social media (15 min per 2-3 of following: Twit FB G+ LI Pin

☐ Promotion strategies/tactics

☐ Publishing progress post/article/book

☐ Other (in exchange for one of the above)

Notes:

_____

_____

_____

The Last Sunday

Meditate. Watch the sun rise. Watch it set. Sit by a body of water. Soak up the songs of birds or laughter of children. Find beauty around you and use it to fuel your next six month goal.

Respite Week 2 Goal Assessment:

☐ maintenance/planning achieved
☐ maintenance/planning partially achieved

What was exciting about everything you achieved in the last six months?

_____

_____

_____

_____

_____

What excites you about your next goal?

_____

_____

_____

_____

_____

ABOUT THE AUTHOR

Alexis Donkin lives in Southern California with her family and real life familiar. She has lived many places and studied many things. She paints, sings, and dances when she's not writing.

If you found this book helpful (or even if you didn't!), **rate and review it**! That is a great way to support authors. Also, be sure to check out Alexis' fiction and nonfiction work and subscribe to her newsletter at http://alexisdonkin.com.

CONNECT ONLINE

Official Website: http://www.alexisdonkin.com
Twitter: https://twitter.com/#!/alexisdonkin
Facebook: https://www.facebook.com/authoralexisdonkin
Blog: http://alexisdonkin.blogspot.com
Smashwords: http://www.smashwords.com/profile/view/alexisdonkin
Patreon: http://www.patreon.com/alexisdonkin